THE INGRAM EXPERIENCE

The Ingram Experience

Awakening

JUSTIN INGRAM-TOWNES

Contents

I dedicate this adventure of awakening to every single being on the planet and beyond.

AWAKENING

5/15/21

<u>Ocean of Love Meditation</u>

I first saw fire both above and beneath a golden ocean of love. I saw the park in North Duarte, where I grew up. I felt pulses of energy in my body. Waves sometimes. I felt Archangel Chamuel and I saw two balls of light that came to see me. I could feel and see the balls of light vibrationally descending down to me as I vibrationally ascended up to meet them. I felt an energy force massage my pained back area. I felt a warm sensation in my left foot, right hand and back, releasing my pain.

<u>1st Reiki Placement Meditation</u>

I saw a bright light that slowly got brighter over time. I saw the star of David, many triangles and pyramids. I felt an energetic pressure on my entire body and it filled me up completely. I felt this energy massage my back. I had a few twitches in my hands and legs and I saw four hands reveal something to me, like it was dropped down from above. They may have been blue. I saw pieces of symbols but no full ones. Also a few incomplete portals. The hands I saw opened like a lotus flower. I also saw a white ceiling above me.

5/16/21

<u>Reiki Level 2 Training Meditation</u>

At first I was walking in a bright forest with super tall trees. Very ethereal. I walked to a side path that led to another side path, that led to a bright, grassy hill. On this hill I saw a bright light from the sky pointed right at me. It fell over me. All around me and lifted me up into it. I saw and felt my clothes fall from me and I was naked in the light, floating. Then a rainbow stream of light started intensely flowing into my third eye. It made my body on Earth shake. I could see different balls of light; Archangel Chamuel, Archangel Gabriel, Archangel Uriel, Archangel Michael. Then I saw an R then an A then I knew RaXa was with me. She is so excited to heal with me!

I also saw faces of beings that were not human, nor did I recognize them. They wanted to tell me something. It was so bright while I was held within the light. I am on the right path! I also saw and felt a pushing and pulling up the plasticity of my mind. It was black, so outside energy is doing that. My hands and feet were very warm and fuzzy. My body was vibrating and I saw places I've never been. Strong waves of energy pulsing into and all through me.

5/25/21
The Aura
The Aura is the densest and most distant part of your energy field. Easiest to heal. Most movable. Chakras are second-most resistant to healing. The body is the most resistant. Each chakra projects out into the layers of the aura.

-
The Chakras
Wheels of energy contained within the body.
First Layer- Root Chakra/First Chakra/Safety/Security/Survival
Second Layer - Sacral Chakra/Emotions and Sexual Relationships
Third Layer - Solar Plexus/Power/Will/Ambition
Fourth Layer - Heart Chakra/Relationships/Family/Self-Love/Unconditional Love

Fifth Layer - Throat Chakra/Communication/Claireaudience/Hearing your Spirit Guides

Sixth Layer - Third Eye Chakra/How do you see the world?/Clairvoyance/Clear Sight/Visions/Connection to the Astral Realm

Seventh Layer - Crown Chakra/Divine Connection/What are you putting out to the world?/Claircognizance/Clear Knowing/Akashic Records

6/5/2021

Last night in my dreams I had new information and light codes downloaded into me. I could feel the information and light flow into me from different dimensions. I'm not sure what the beings upgrading me we're doing specifically, but I could sense I am now more enhanced and connected than before. The nameless light of the Sun is now within me. I also remember meeting a girl with hair like mine, lighter skin. Very nice. I let her follow me through a tunnel maze of a room/building complex and she followed me until we reached the end. Who was she?

6/10/2021

I have awoken my GOLDEN DIAMOND RAINBOW RAY. I HAVE FUSED WITH MY SHADOW-SELF AND GAINED THE POWER OF ILLUMINATION!

I started to spin counter-clockwise while holding the Palo Santo and the Sage from the Sacred Mountain and I could see the universes as I broke myself free from these generational curses and entrapments. I am free!

I AM NÜ

6/11/2021

Wow! So much happened yesterday! I lit my candles and smudged the room. Then I was called to make a crystal grid with all of my skulls. Intuitively I started adding more crystals until they had all been placed together resembling a Sun with 7 rays. I kept my Ruby in my pocket and Ragnarok (my Auralite-23 crystal skull dragon) around my neck. He stayed with me the entire time. So protective!

I laid down and started with a New Moon Solar Eclipse Meditation. During the meditation my stomach really started to hurt and I felt compelled to rip the golden twin-flame cord from my Solar Plexus. It hurt as I wrenched the cord from my bodies (physical & energetic). I then planted the cord into the ground and let the earth take it and give it back. After the meditation ended, I played angelic high-frequency awakening sounds for two hours. This is when I confronted my shadow.

I was portaling inwards and I kept seeing a singular eye looking at me. I realized my shadow-self was hiding and needed to be located. I found it in the "in-between realm", when you close your eyes halfway. He attacked me with fear, anger, sadness, worry, hatred and betrayal. I chose to unconditionally love him and I drank him in. He accepted, thinking he would destroy me from the inside-out.

As my shadow filled my being, I started to shine my internal light which started to illuminate every part of my shadow. After full illumination was reached, the shadow disappeared and within the shadow was my inner-child. Just laying there in a fetal position, in defensive-mode with a scorpion deity stabbing it's poison tail at everything, trying to make all the pain stop. I picked up my inner-self and lifted him up into a Golden Love Ray with me. I told him I love him no matter what and I will always be here forever! I then hugged my inner-child and he absorbed into my Heart Chakra and the light spectrum that emanated from within me is my newly awakened Golden Diamond Rainbow Ray of Illumination. I can call on it whenever I want because it is within me.

I have successfully fused with my shadow-self, who was really my wounded inner-child. Reverse-exorcism complete! It took every one of my crystals to help because my shadow is me and has my strength, but it didn't have my light. I was also given my new Spirit Light Name. I am NÜ!

An Eclipse is the perfect time to locate, confront, heal and fuse with your inner-child. Bringing that type of "dark" energy within and transmuting it into Golden Diamond Rainbow Energy is one of the most powerful things you can do! Demand your freedom and take back-control of your light! All is possible!

6/17/21

During my crystal skull meditation with "White Eyes" (my traveler crystal skull), I met a being named GARGLOG who is a jellyfish being. It lives on a planet of complete water. The species is highly intelligent and can exist outside of water. But if they go outside water, their bodies turn ethereal. They cannot have a physical body outside water. He was/is a Blue Jellyfish from Nebula Six, in the fifth dimension. He told me to speak with Metatron and please do as he requests and read the Keys of Enoch because it has been too long that I've waited. It is time and necessary.

He loves me and his family loves me. I used to know him and that's why he made himself readily available for my purchase online. He says he has a lot to tell me about how his dimension of people work and operate. He can astral travel and upon entering water he can condense into his polymorphous form that is made up of the same jellyfish body material. He can regenerate and they live 600 years generally. He invites me to astral project to his planet to have multiple downloads.

3/25/21
Previous Journal Entry
Does our Third Eye summon portals? They show themselves to me sideways sometimes.

3/27/21
Previous Journal Entry
Today I was invited to a desert party with my good friend. He had friends who all accept me with open arms. They all hugged me "hello" and I'm super excited for tonight. Thank you universe!

3/28/21
Previous Journal Entry
I was a part of a Shaman Ceremony! I was given a message from the Shaman. "Be proud of yourself! You are amazing! You've done an amazing job Justin and I love you. Hold your head up high like you used to! You are equal to everyone else. Everyone is equal to you. We are all divine spirits living a human experience. If people who treat you bad and are mean to you, they just don't understand. They are ignorant! Focus on the future and build that into what you want it to be. Don't stay stuck in the past where people hurt you. Let it go and live in the present. Have faith in Spirit and the fact that we are all children of Spirit and everything you need will always come when you need it. You are worthy. Take up your crown and king yourself!"

6/24/21

<u>Trip Log</u>

6:15 PM: I found one Blue Cloud. My intentions for the experience is to connect with my crystal skulls on the deepest level possible, connect with my crystals and expand my super-consciousness! I only wish to speak with beings of the light!

1:38 AM I realize how galactic our eyes are. We can see the entire universe when viewing "space" and "outer-space."

6/25/21

<u>Trip Review</u>

So this time I started to play Native American healing songs. The orange glow of the candle light was used by Archangel Melchizedek to run new energy through my Sacral Chakra. I cried a lot and realized I don't want to let my ex-girlfriend go, but I should because it weighs me down.

I called on Archangels Haniel, Uriel and Metatron to help guide me. Arizona is the mission. I was eye-gazing with myself in the mirror and I connected with "Third Eye Me." I gazed with the moon and I saw the light projections of the moon's reflection multidimensionally. I could see the moon without my glasses!

I was scrying into my crystal skull "EXCELSIOR" and I could see and feel my thoughts and memories turn into small, incremental, digitally-thought-formed information and it was deposited into the skull. I was meditating inside of Excelsior while this happened. I now know how to deposit information into a clear quartz crystal skull!

Before falling asleep I listened to a dragon meditation and I met my guardian dragon. His name is GRIGGORIO and his colors are white, blue, silver and green. So his energy is divine, water, alchemical and healing. He took me up and away to the dragon realm.

7/2/21
Trip Log
5:00 PM: I found a White Cloud. My intentions are to fully unlock my energy reading and seeing powers. I want to see the energy of my crystals and crystal skulls. I want guidance on how to keep my powers unlocked! I also want to see my inner-self!

8:00PM: I saw and felt a new awakening of a light spectrum from within. I saw Mayan priests and headdresses. I saw the lineage of the inner-people who accept me as their own. The Wolf People call out to me. I was a main guardian of an ancient crystal skull. There is an entrance to Mount Shasta that will be open for me if I believe enough to go. I will be met with a guide to the Inner-Earth.

I can feel other beings within me. In my core it has awakened. It hurt for a while, mainly in my arms, but after the light codes were done awakening the dormant parts of my being, I am now much more whole. I am stronger, smarter, more cunning than before.

-
Telepathy
Beings who teleport, first master their minds. Telepathy before teleportation. A master network that all minds on Earth can access like a worldwide web of telepathically linked individuals who, through this pattern can instantly communicate with each other whenever needed. Once this is achieved, the collective thought will create a light gateway that has access to the mind to project itself through the lights to go anywhere!

Accessing Crystals

To access a crystal one must gaze upon it for two minutes. Devote your attention and being to the crystal and acknowledgment of its sentientness. When an agreement has made between the crystal being in the individual, open and connect to your Heart Chakra to the crystal and it secrets shall be revealed!

Teleportation

To teleport you must, with your mind, deconstruct your physical form into light codes that attach to the surrounding ascending or descending light transport and you travel with the light as one and you reconstruct your body starting with your consciousness.

7/4/21

Trip Review

After about an hour, which I spent smudging the room and listening to my metaphysical development class meditation music, the Native music started playing and I went into trance and started crying instantly. Then after the release, I saw the light codes and transmissions blasting me. I was being teleported all over the multiverse and I saw Mayan symbols, hieroglyphs, and I saw my past life as a Mayan priest. I was in charge of communication with our crystal skulls and I will find it again soon. Then I felt a pressure on my arms that became uncomfortable. And then saw light scanning my body and changing it structured into a crystalline one. Lady Togepi (the Shaman spirit within my Rose Quartz crystal skull) showed herself to me as well as Metatron.

7/12/21

I just woke up in Arizona and I'm feeling very hopeful. I cried a little because I was hit with an overwhelming loneliness. I've never been on my own like this before and it is a lot. I am going to do a bit of yoga, then head out to a Starbucks for some chai tea. I miss my family and friends. I'm going to park here in Cottonwood for yoga, then I'm going to a crystal shop. I also want to check out the local health food market. I want to make new friends today. I went to two crystal shops and I got info on what direction to head. Yayy!

7/13/21

Day two in Sedona. I feel so much better than I did yesterday morning. Yesterday I went to Starbucks and then in my panic, I signed up for a meditation class online. That calmed me down a little. Then I decided to go and try to meet people that work at crystal shops.

The first one was a rock shop that was owned by an older lady. I got a Garnet, a piece of Hanksite and a Unakite necklace. These new vibrations gave me confidence to head to a crystal shop in Sedona. At the first one I met a lady with short orange hair named Loli. She reminded me of an old friend named Rin. I got a suggestion to come back Wednesday to talk to someone named Fry.

I went to another crystal shop and met Kate who was nice. She told me about the Stupas. While looking for the Sedona Visitor Center I found a sound healing shop where I will be getting a Sacred Drum sound healing. The owner suggested a few healing food stores I could go to.

Next I went looking for more crystal shops and accidentally found the Mecca of crystal shops. There I found info on vortexes and Linda offered me a job! Then I went to Crystal Gratitude and the owner is a Reiki master and told me about all of these great food places. Vegan and gluten-free! I then headed to uptown Sedona and walked around by myself. It was nice meeting locals. Then I came home for the five-elements meditation. It was very calming and grounding. I ate a burrito bowl for dinner!

7/13/21

Journal Entry

I just left the White Light Crystal Shop. The owner increased my Chakra Auras to 15 feet from 6 to 12 inches. Then he told me about the lower Chakras; Seed, Asgard, Midgard & Obsidian. Angel Energy waves went through my body! I am going to the Airport Mesa Vortex now. Then lunch and a movie.

So lunch went very well! The server Jerry is from LA and I definitely put some concepts in his mind to start his awakening process. Then I stopped at Sedona Healing Arts, which was nice but I didn't feel any vibes. So I went next-door to the Flower of Life Shop and I met Lota. He was super-open and understanding of my situation. Lota may be the "Soul Brother" I was told I would meet out in Arizona. He seemed willing to promote me and gave me some info and suggestions! Thank you Archangels for continuing to guide me!

Oh yeah! The Reiki masters are offering classes in Oden Reiki and offered me a free healing next week! He also said every 12 hours we need to recertify with our angels and guides and ask and open up to help constantly because the spirit timer resets every 12 hours! Tomorrow I meet with Fry! I also want to sign up for a reading with Desert Dragon!

7/15/22

<u>Journal Entry</u>

Yesterday I woke up, got ready, got some Starbucks and went straight to Crystal Magic Crystal Shop to see if Fry is working. He wasn't there but he will be on Thursday. I ended up buying a piece of Ulexite! Such an amazing Stone! Then I went to White Lake Crystals and decided to do the Oden Reiki classes next week. I went to Crystal Gratitude to see Tim and instead I met Pam! She introduced me to Prana Healing which is the teachings of Buddha! I got lunch at Picazzos again and talked to mom. I played the past-life regression meditation cd and passed out! So wild. I got a pizza and went to sleep.

7/16/21

<u>Journal Entry</u>

Yesterday I woke up, cleaned, showered, then I went to star-bees. I decided to drive to Phoenix, AZ to get Syrus (my ball python) two small rats. It was one hour and thirty minutes each way and it was one long, fun, beautiful dance party! When I got back to Sedona I wanted to go to the Stone Age Center. The man inside was quite nice but I could tell he was all about the sale. I traversed into the Shamanic Healing Center and met Henry, who invited me to their sound healing concert. I bought a ticket and went. It was so amazing! I also made two friends who moved here two weeks ago. I'm finding my soul tribe! Thank you guides and angels!

I woke up feeling hopeful that I am on the path I was meant to be on. I did my Goshen meditation and prayed to Archangel Melchizedek and I have a drum healing at 11:30 AM. What will happen? Then I am going to sign up for Oden Reiki. I'm really excited for today! I was told about some ecstatic dance tonight, which should be wonderful. Maybe I'll meet my future wife there. Or maybe I already met her. I want to get in a serious committed relationship!

Last night during the Shamanic Healing Ceremony I saw two huge hands doing the Mudra of the Buddha. Then I saw the wooden statue of Buddha from the Stupa!

During the sacred drumming ceremony, I felt my astral body slipping beneath the crust of the Earth. I floated down to a cavern lit up by fire light and there were hands waiting for me that cushioned by descent. They kept repeating "We have been waiting so long for you." Then I saw myself with a wolf head and a fur cape as I chanted and danced to the drumming. I also saw two moving quicksilver streams made of iron going to my Third Eye. I also learned a new equilibrium technique from this Shaman.

7/26/21

Today I start the water fast that my guides and Angels requested of me. I woke up at 5:22 AM ready to take on the world. I'm about to light an incense, perform my morning routine, do some yoga, choose a Sedona vortex, shower and then it's time to head over to Sedona. It's been exactly two weeks since I left home in California and moved here. I love it at this point. I feel like I've been here for two months! I want to stay as long as needed for me to learn all of Oden Reiki and see what happens channeling-wise. I'm going to take the psychic development classes today. "Body-of-Glass" and "How to Channel." See you on the other side!

7/13/21

Previous Journal Entry

Airport Mesa Vortex. Angels say "Justin we are so happy you made it to Arizona. You made it! You will channel our information so that all can reach their true enlightened purpose. The goal is to reach the state of singular consciousness. To reach wholeness. Anything you want you shall receive Justin. You took the perceived risk of coming here and the singularity of what you have done will become a multiplicical awareness expansion. Who do you want to be? What do you want? Ask for it. Manifest it! Feel it! Be it! Love it now, not later.

The Inner-Earth people are waiting for me.

7/13/21
Previous Journal Entry

Your beliefs literally create your reality. Based off of what you believe, people form their own beliefs about you, themselves, everything in your awareness. The web of beliefs formats the network of all individuals gathered in any given area. We are made of our beliefs. They shape our realities and the individuals involved in our universe. Locality matters but as a whole we are all connected in this way.

7/17/21
Previous Journal Entry

Say every day - "I expect magic today" and if you expect it, it will happen.

7/27/21
Day 2 Water Fast

I woke up at 5:22 AM again today. The Grand Canyon was very interesting! I figured out that I still have people in my life I need to detox out of my mind. Past hurt, past memories. They all are exiting my mind so I can move forward. I broke last night and ate a little bit but it's OK. I'm just going to keep going forward. Something is telling me to trip today and I shall heed the call! It isn't hard drinking only water...it just sucks flavor-wise and is boring. While not eating I have so much time and energy to do everything and anything I want! Let's go day-two water fast wooo!! Today I'm going to the Boynton Canyon Vortex. Blu-ray one!

7/27/21

Today's Downloads

I met Pachamama and she helped me with my Pharaoh Ramses II past life regression. My left side is my Pharaoh side. The Ingram Experience.

7/28/21

Etophogy Dreams

I made a double "Monad David" tetrahedron and placed it in all directions around myself as well as the Metatron's Cube. Then I imagined a thick golden blanket over my bed and placed my body in a five-pointed-star formation. My eyes started fluttering and I could see many, many light orbs surrounding me. I asked to bring all of my past lives, especially my pharaoh lives back into this body and reality and then I saw the sky and clouds with a bright light behind the cloud. Then I saw feet and sandals walking. I asked for this being to show me more of itself and I saw a being with a face I cannot explain because it was multi-dimensional. After that I fully fell asleep. My left arm still has this intense, powerful aching feeling from when I connected with Pachamama and she let me feel the ocean on the red rock from my past lives.

RAMSES II

7/28/21

Day 3 Water Fast

Today I woke up at 4:41 AM which I have been seeing every-where. Last night I almost broke and got a pizza but I resisted and went to sleep. I woke up feeling delirious and tired inside of myself but drinking the moon water helps me feel better. I had a dream that my gods and ancestors came to see me and they were glowing colors like the gods in Mulan and Her-cules. Bright blues, pinks, yellows, greens and purples. They all wanted to meet me and asked why I didn't have a White Shaman help me and what was my perceived relationship to the Asian culture. They were some of my other lifetimes I have lived. So amazing! My guides. There were so many.

7/29/21

Day Four Water Fast

Yesterday I went to Diamond Point with Michael and found so many crystals! Herkimer Payson diamonds. I also ate dinner because the hike made me feel like I was going to die. Water fast reset today! Today I may go to Bell Rock Vortex and see what channels through me. I think plant medicines are definitely my tool for increasing the communications between otherworldly beings and myself. I think the weekends are packed with people so maybe Cathedral Rock today instead. I'm excited!

7/27/21

Downloads

I watched how Boynton Canyon's energy vortexes infuse people with passionate sexual energy and motivational energy. Ideas flourish and upon leaving, The Kachina Woman in the mountain showed me a past life in the ocean and then I saw the Sphinx! Then I blasted forward under the Sphinx through these geometrical, white tunnels. Instantly I was in a bright room with everyone wearing white and looking at me. I am Pharaoh Ramses the Second!

During the transmission, all of the priests and priestesses were watching me lay down in a granite box while I teleported to another dimension...another Universe. Then that lifetime was channeled back into my body and bodies through my left arm. My left arm is my pharaoh and power arm. I can call Cosmic and Earth energy into my palm and palms and either throw the energy into another person or infuse it into myself for more energy. The transfer hurt my arm really bad but I'll be OK.

7/30/21
Trip Log
8:18 AM: I enjoyed some chocolates and viewed the Taj Mahal. I intend to meet the Wolf People, my ancestors, my tribe!

9:25 AM: I have reached the top of the mountain. Now it is time to go within...
Also a dragonfly is up here perched right next to me.

-
Downloads
We are one facet of the dodecahedron. Each side is a Universe. Not parallel. All existing at once as a phase of The All. Multiple dodecahedrons exist.

-
From the Wolf People
"Bring everyone on the surface facing one another as brothers. Brotherhood. The pack. We are one. Teach. Preach. Build. They will come to you as their leader. Their leader of the Sun. Harness the Sun like Goku with his spirit bomb in each palm of your hands. The power is harnessed as you will it. Don't

forget LOVE is the way forward. We will speak soon. The Sun has chosen you my Son. Love always."

– Wolf

I spoke with Oden, the Sun, the Wolf People and the Nagas.
There is a tetrahedron on every side of the dodecahedron. The dodecahedron has twelve five-sided faces. It is at the center of Metatron's cube.

Angels and other beings without bodies always present themselves to you in the same way. That's how you know who it is and if you instead projected an illusion of your own mind.

Quetzalcoatl

8/2/21
I woke up at 5:20 AM and handled a few relationship ending texts and now I am at Cathedral Rock Vortex. I am super excited! Time to get Galactic!

8/2/21
Trip log
7:53 AM: I found one Blue Cloud and the galaxy is calling me. I am currently listening to a powerful Kali mantra to remove enemies and black magic.

8:59 AM: Age is irrelevant to anything. I have been shown that no matter if one is younger or older, it is just a body. How old is your soul? Where were you last? Who are you? These are the important questions. The vortex speaks. I'm sitting at the base of a vortex tree, gaining insights and symbols of our future.

-

Cathedral Spirit of Vortex

All who come are changed. The energetic force contained within your physical body can be changed for it is water, as is this universe. Bodies of water to be charged and ignited. Quickened and slowed. Increased or decreased. You're drawn here to heal and discover. Love one another.

Open your heart fully to give and accept love as a currency. No more negativity

We tend to see ourselves from an individualistic standpoint.

But we are all one, from one source, the all, which contains us all in our various forms and modalities. Together we move forward. Against one another causes stagnation.

I feel very rejuvenated and forward thinking. Allowing old attachments to leave me. LEAVE ME! They are gone and so it is!

"Everything that has happened so far has gotten me to where I am. All is a part of the journey. Every decision, every failure, every success, it is all to move us forward. Forgive yourself, Justin, forgive yourself for everything you have ever done! We are the Angels here for you always. You are way too hard on yourself. As your mission is revealed, the path forward shall illuminate for you. No more worrying about anything."

-

The Sun

Prepare, for I am going to increase 20° in the next five years. I will increase in size and temperature as time moves. In order for more advanced species and civilizations to exist, I must increase my output. 1000% I will increase. But so will your capacity to withstand and understand ME. New life is coming. NEW CONSCIOUSNESS NOW!!!

The tetrahedron and Mogan David all exist within the face of the dodecahedron.

Multifaceted light codes existing as a multiplex of activations all at once. All at the same time. The multiplexity of time and existence.

All shapes within Metatron's Cube or essentials to the proliferation of life on a planet. It starts with the elements and continues into multiplexity.

The Ant People

They wish to speak to me. They are the givers. They are the BUILDERS. I see faces in Cathedral Rock; Mayan Ancestors. This was an ocean with many inhabitants. The Ant People are still here. We are one of the six tribes of Inner Earth people. We are here to give you strength. We are ARCTURIANS!

We are the ANTIGUA people. We are Arcturians descended into physical human bodies. We call ourselves ANT because the ant is the most solid and reliable builder on Earth1. We do as we please while also building for our culture, our society, our queen, our way of life. Teach our ways of unity and oneness to all on the surface. As above, so below.

8/3/21

In my dream I kept out-running/out-flying an "Ice God." I have the power of ice within me. It needs to be unlocked.

8/4/21

Today I decided to go find a Native drum. I drove to uptown Sedona and let myself be guided. I found a small shop with only one vegan drum for $197 and it was the only vegan drum I could find. I will go get it soon. I then called a man named Nova and he directed me to The Kachina House. I discovered many different Kachinas that really spoke to me. I shall retrieve some soon! I want to see The Sacred Drum Shamans and they sold me on a stone I can't remember the name of. It is 3.5 billion years old and looks like a piece of chocolate. I went to see the movie "Old" and it was a good time.

I woke up from a nap to a text from J saying that J was sick physically and was throwing up blood. He asked if I could bring myself to the house to do Oden Reiki. I shot over there to help. During the healing ceremony I portaled 55 demonic entities into 55 of the Payson Diamonds and buried them outside. I felt very in-tune and accomplished when I was done. Afterwards I was approached by "friends" from the retreat and we all hit it off. I was able to open their minds and now they want more. I am a galactic shamanistic Pharaoh!

8/16/21

Butte Vortex

Just because I break contact after a portal has been opened, activated and gone through, does not mean the portal is closed. The portals I use to contact beings without bodies must be closed after I open my eyes because they can still be accessed by other humans. When pening a portal, move it counter-clockwise. To close a portal, move it clockwise.

I just spoke with the Spider People. They have 4 arms and are masters of energetic webs and are descendants of the

Giants. This is why they're able to have more limbs than other humanoids. They have the ability to create a poisonous liquid that breaks down what it touches on an elemental level.

-
Daily Galactic Affirmation from the Galactic Calendar
I dedicate in order to evolve.

Universalizing synchronicity.

I seal the matrix of navigation with the crystal tone of cooperation.

I am a Galactic activation portal – enter me!

8/9/21
Chapel of the Holy Cross Vortex
I woke at 5:57AM: What I realized here is to not take life too seriously. Relax, figure out what I want, love and forgive myself and others, go with the flow and believe in myself and the Universe. Everything is always working out for me, best-case scenario. I always have more than enough money coming in! Thank you Supreme Being! Thank you Ganesh! Thank you Archangels! Thank you Universe! I love you! I love everyone!

As soon as I was done journaling and praying, a new acquaintance called and said they have an opening at the mansion and it would be paid for just so I can move in and start healing professionally! Then in the afternoon I met up with another acquaintance at my favorite new restaurant and we talked and she offered me a room at her house in Sedona. Thank you Angels, guides, Ancestors and spirits! Thank You Universe!

8/10/21
I woke up today to the sound of my neighbor's blender. I'm glad though because I had a 10-episode nightmare and it directly correlated with my big decision of where I will move.

Either to the Village in Sedona or to San Diego with my new friends...

So it's 8:18 PM and I'm all in my feelings. I'm feeling more nostalgic than anything. I am feeling the energetic shifts into another reality. I haven't heard from the girls I met so I'm guessing the roommate wasn't down to live with a man, but I totally understand. So that means my Angels are saying, "Go to San Diego for the next part of your adventure!" One-hundred percent to infinity and beyond! An exploration of space! I'll update tomorrow before I get on the road.

8/11/21

I just woke up for the last time in Cottonwood. At my Airbnb. This was literally the most magical time in my life. I know who I am. I am me! I am loved. I am worthy! I am amazing! Thank you!

8/13/22

Friday the 13th

Wow! Today I woke up in San Diego! I am so blessed! Thank you so much guides, Angels and spirits! I am enough! Today I might take a trip with my new friends. I haven't told anyone where I live yet. I want my privacy so I'm setting boundaries. I am happy!

8/18/21

So I know it's been a while since I last journaled, but I've been integrating everything and creating another solid foundation. I am treated so well here. A new bed is coming and I changed my room. Today I may do a video...if I feel like it!

8/19/21

Hello world! I just woke up super full. I'm going to stop eating before bed. My dream world has been gnarly so I want to go in as clean as possible. I've ended all unhealthy relationships and I just moved into a new room. I love it here. My new bed is coming today and I'm really excited about that! I'm gonna go get some coffee in Sedona and plan on what new products I will create. Probably sound bath and drumming videos along with Chakra-opening and clearing videos. Thank you Guides and Angels for everything. I love you all so much! Thank you for my beautiful soulmate!

8/21/21

Hello! I've been feeling empty lately and I don't know why. I think I have been wanting an intense, deep love relationship with my twin flame. I will focus on work and building my brand so I can start financially doing what I need to do. Meditating needs to come back into my life.

8/27/21

My life is so super different now. I'm living in San Diego now and my life is amazing! I have everything I want and more! All my manifestations are coming true. The last thing is my soulmate. I'm still getting ready for when I meet her and everything makes sense. Thank you!

8/31/21

Today is the last day of August. Tomorrow we are going to the unofficial "Burning Man" and I'm quite nervous. It will be very spiritual for me because I will be fasting again. Water and juice fasting for sure. I still feel lonely in San Diego but I can feel my soulmate coming closer. I want a true love that will last as long as it is supposed to. I want to raise a cat, puppy, and a child with a wife figure.

9/9/21

<u>Sleep Talk</u>

The blue person within. If I send my blue form into a person's being it will fill them with the Blu-Ray and heal them. We all have a blue light activation light code body who can hop or phase through timelines to bring healing to each self. The blue-self is the emotional body who never dies and thinks all lifetimes are the same one. Therefore it can be summoned to each timeline to complete the Galactic Healing. Blu-Ray One!

-

<u>Blue-Ray Activation Meditation</u>

As you call on the blue energy and it fills you from the top down, let it fully channel into you. Let yourself glow from the inside out.

9/9/21

Before I wake up I am in a dream world of information. I can bring this information back to my body but as I write it out, I start to forget. If I go back to sleep I can access the information again and repeat the cycle until all the information has been received.

9/14/21

I am so grateful, thankful and happy! Everything I ever wanted is coming to me. Love, happiness, understanding and abundance. All of it is flowing into my life with such candor that it has taken some time to adjust but I am now fully aware and living in this timeline. Thank you so much Ganesha! I love you so much. Thank you for always being with me!

9/15/21

Last night I slept on my Crystal Bible and I can feel my mind absorbing the information and knowledge into itself at an exponential rate! It was as if I were still asleep in my body but my mind was awake!

You are worthy! Take up your crown and king yourself!

4/18/21
Previous Journal Entry
Fear literally hold you back. Every time you jump back into fear, avoid something, procrastinate. Fear is literally and physically holding you back. Literally!

4/20/21
Previous Journal Entry
In my dreams I meet a being who looks like me who you don't want to be like and doesn't teach you anything. You can only exist and think minimum thoughts when around this being. It seems like a trickster because it smiles and trolls a lot. It only speaks mentally. I don't like its vibe but it's a place to stay outside of time. It can't change into any other form than what it already is. It also isn't very nice. You can ask questions but it probably won't answer. There's no writing system. You can only ask questions but you won't always get an answer because it is not nice. You have to mentally create your own spaceship or hope your friends hear your telepathic scream to be let out of the planet. We stay away from it but I am not afraid. I almost beat its system last night. I'll figure out how to do things on its planet.

-

Dream World
I have locks. Limitless art. Dark mushroom web that we add the dark energy into and as a group we transmit the energy into light then we go to the next level. Remember not to stick your tongue out in this world. The energy transfer of ions is inconsequential. I star walk everywhere. There were three

different levels of dark matter transmutation. It was put inside of a brontosaurus shaped plasticky husk. It went through our chests and bodies. We work it through the creation and then we keep moving through the dream state.

9/24/21

I have experienced so many ups and downs. I've gotten lost into the matrix again but I am slowly coming back to my own real reality. Things are seemingly difficult but I always remember...I wrote all of this!

-

<u>Dream World</u>

I am in this black space. There are quadrupeds here who are humanoid but they bend over, very tall and walk on all fours. I change my body, which is ethereal into black space with golden stars. Then those around me change to this color frequency energy and are healed. I program my internal universal body with a healing intention and color and then everyone is permeated by it and I completely healed. I program my body to heal specific issues and then I pull it into my being and put the program into all around me for massive healings or personal healings.

9/26/21

<u>Dream World</u>

Imagine the Zodiac as a map and we live in-between the lines. Names have degrees here. In this dimension I see the zodiac wheel of 12. My site zooms in close to what looks like black ink and then I can see and feel beings living in the in-between. They all have names with degrees. I was in the time of Leo and yesterday morning I was literally in Sagittarius!

9/28/21

Dream World

As I travel through this dreamworld I become elements and heal through them. I became air and healed. I became water and healed. Every thought and action heals myself and anyone within my field of awareness. As I move through space I can do anything and I chose to alchemize. What is my connection to the Sami Shaman? They become one with the elements and speak with her elemental essence to further healing. Time to learn, explore and train.

9/30/21

Dream World

I am a battery that gets charged up by light to heal those with ether energy.

10/2/21

Dream World

Fenrir the Dragon. I go to the same three or four places in my dreams every single night.

10/3/21

Dream World

I was back in the dream at the island school surrounded by water. When I woke up I could see different versions of Metatron's cube. Different sizes, different angles. I think I use Metatron's Cube to portal out of my body and to return back. Drawing Metatron's cube opens the portal to anywhere I want to go!

The Mountain

I found myself driving up the winding path to the mountain. I have come absolutely full circle. I have left my home, gone to

Sedona, moved to San Diego and now I am back here. Sitting and writing about this amazing life.

I am feeling highly emotional and I must be releasing but I am really craving a deep connection. I want to be with best friends and you know what? Thank you Ganesh for guiding me to the most fulfilling love and work relationship with my life partner! I love, love, love you!

Angel Question From The Top Of The Mountain. "What Do I Do Next?"

"Fully awaken all of your abilities! Retrieve all of your soul so you can fully awaken all of your abilities. Fully awake and all of your abilities so you can spread the word of what you learn and experience. You are ready to write about these experiences the characters have because the characters are you! As you grow and learn, so do the characters. Start when you get back to San Diego, after you awaken your mask and peer into the Sami Shaman crystal ball.

This is the imprint of the Sun. The Sun wishes life and love on us. The Sun infuses its light with love and the frequency of love allows life to grow and form because sunlight is a form of attention concentrated into a light being. The Sun, by extension, is touching us, healing us with love and attention. The Sun loves us all unconditionally. The Sun is shining. Love the Sun. The Sun is a portal to God. God is change. God is inertia.

Inertia

Propulsion and acceleration forward without slowing down unless an outside force influences the desired trajectory.

10/5/21

Last night I found a Blue Cloud, then received my crystal ball. The transmission came through to me. Find us – Sami people. I am a Sami Shaman and I am to find my people and learn the old ways of which I have forgotten but I shall remember.

10/7/21

Trip Log

I accessed "Shaman Mode" today at 11:01AM. My intentions are to connect and release with my Sami Shaman heritage. To converse with my Preseli mask and with BERGAMOT, my Atlantisite dragon. Also I will be speaking with Ganesh, my love. I will also be calling in my true love soulmate forever love. She is coming...no more hiding! Be what you want!

10/8/22

Yesterday the trip only lasted about two hours. I used the crystal ball and secret password to activate my generational healing. I understood that I don't need to know why people treat me how they do. I will be happiest focusing on myself. I am what matters. Love and light to all.

10/10/21

I was in a vortex portal blasting forward. It is changing me through the winds of life. In the winds and sands of time, I take care of the what and the why, the Universe takes care of the "how." Trust in it. It set up this entire trip for me to meet the people I need to meet for my intense and amazing future.

10/12/22

I have been waking up and falling back into the same dream reams. One is the ocean scenes. This time I was far in the water.

I was at the party scene realm, then living with many other roommates with many bedrooms and relationships going on. I remember feeling many things in these dreams.

10/13/22

So I've been dealing with certain people who are trying to control my mind. They are weaker mentally and don't understand my secrets. I'm so much stronger mentally than I have ever been!

10/15/22

As I sit here in the desert, after my meditation, I feel so content and ready to step into my Reiki Master teacher role. I am so thankful for my happy, eager to learn, respectful, powerful, understanding, passionate, loving, honorable students.

10/14/21

Dream World

Before I fell asleep I saw Metatron's cube and when I woke up the sunlight shines through my eyelids and I see these patterns that are spinning, creating portal vortexes that bring me back into my body.

10/15/22

Now is the time to embrace my truest, fullest, highest self. I am NÜ! I AM RAMSES II! I AM POWERFUL. I AM ME! I expect magic today and every day. I expect miracle upon miracle. I am love unconditional! Thank you Oden. Thank you Ganesh!

10/20/21

Within cells interlink. Lucy unlocks powers the deeper you go. Three deep. Blue Clouds.

10/21/21

I just did Desert Dragon's Inner-Temple meditation. It was made of Preseli Bluestone. Archangel Metatron came to see me and let me know that all the powers and abilities I seek are already inside of me. He then left me with a staff of Golden Diamond with a crystal Metatron's Cube on top with a silver light that shines in all directions once activated. This is my rod, my staff of knowledge, my Yggdrasil branch. I am to use it wisely or it shall phase to another who would use it righteously in the service of the universe.

Dream World

Through causation and allocation I heal. I found you through my own visions of the future. My past life love is returning to me now. Through time-space and dimensions. Come to me!

10/26/21

My birthday/solar return is soon. I'm feeling quite strange and I know I need to find three Clouds soon. Either today, tomorrow or Thursday. Last week at "EveryWhen" I did a DMT meditation for the second time and I was taken to the realm/dimension of color and I was color-washed with every gradient of light that exists. Blessings showered through me by the Golden Gods with no faces.

Dream Transmission

Justin, you come from the Andromeda galaxy. Andromeda Five as a Pleiadian as well. Now we are now making this part of your heritage known. We love you from the galactic ship we wait for you in. Find a piece of crystal you will use to communicate with us. Speak to us at night before and after you wake up. Intend to speak with us and it shall be an instant communication. We love you so much and we are looking forward to speaking with you and enhancing your love frequency. Love always

– The Pleiadians

10/27/21

My Will has increased one-hundred fold. What I think, I feel and experience in both the dreamworld and in the real 3-D. I can put any healing gradient of light through any being. You are now healed. I am now healed. I love you. Go in light and love. Pleiadian. Andromeda Six.

10/28/21

We all want to love. What is love? Multi-dimensional pure acceptance of life force energy funneled through our being like an asteroid belt being guided into creation.

-

Dream World

While in the middle-way I can choose to go deeper into my crystals or I can pull back into my body. The choice is mine. Who are all of the beings I continue to interact with in my dreams? The city island wants to be written about.

When and where do our Third Eye dragons come from? Auralite 23! Personal dragon?

10/28/21

Trip Log

Today I found three Blue Clouds at 12:22 PM. I intend to meet my Pleiadian family, create the structure of my future here on Urantia and to more fully awaken and understand my psychic powers and abilities.

"We are here to grow and know. To know and show. To show and flow. To flow and grow. To grow and know..."

Honey is created to be used and consumed. The honey does not resist or regret this. It is why the honey is here!

-The Spirit of all Bees

The power and the magic of mirror reflections. Without these tools, how can one do complete shadow work, dimensional work, eye gazing. It becomes a task that without a mirror, we must rely on nature to reflect this back. Don't be afraid of the black mirror!

I see the Star. The Star is the portal. I am the Star. I am Star. I am Portal. I am NÜ

-

Saraphim
The Beings whos being sets the tone of those who listen's tonal frequency of love. We are Pleidian.

A child wants to be seen. Who is the child? Who is the child? She must be brought in very specifically. Preparation is almost complete...

I am Andromedan. I will communicate when it is time.

I sealed myself within myself and I can unseal it as I wish. This is a seal of safety and security for the lower three chakras. Seal of time and space.

-

Daily Schedule
-Wake up
-Give thanks

-Remember Andromeda!

I just met a microscopic being on my glasses and I loved them so much and now they are gone. Thank you for being!

It starts with a V

Intention is everything is attention
I have found infinity. Infinity starts at the point. The deviation. V
What is the point?
A destination...Point?
A point is really a vortex portal used to get from point A to point B.

We time travel through points. A point is a culmination space where time and space must comply. We are the manifesters and we are communicating to you through an inflection point. Use these to communicate.

Teach through nature comparisons.
Different ways of seeing.
I am a literal vehicle of light.
I am the inflection point.
I am that "point" in time and space.
I have found my point.
The point is you!

Seen from the perspective of the "point"...
I can access all space/time/all knowledge/gematria
Crystals hold all knowledge.
Access the necessary points within and no...
Key is necessary.

Hold it within and they can only wish to behold the glory of the Rainbow Light

What you behold...is all in your eyes. The owl
Everything we do is our offering.
Everything matters
Don't forget
YOU matter

10/29/21
Dream World
Welcome back Justin. The galactic upgrade you experienced in the 5D will awaken your abilities further. You are a beautiful pink and blue Pleidian soul and love is what we are. Follow the V.

-Plieadians

10/29/21
After Log: The Power of 3
Experiencing the power of three was amazing. This is what happened. I learned to teach using nature comparisons. If I jump on and become a vibration of a Being or color, I can tell my skin to match the vibration like a chameleon. My transformation powers are activating as well. I saw beautiful color blankets that I moved with my mind and then I cleaned out my Third Eye with my Golden Diamond Rainbow broom. Then with it cleaned, I unlocked my Third Eye with intention and Metatron's cube. I created a second dimensional/3D energetic love Being that now exists in my room.

I connected with my future daughter who told me to name her Andy preferably. I fused with my Lyran cat-self and heritage. Andromeda the star system is one of my homes. I am of the Seraphim. The Seraphim by way of Archangel Michael, Archangel Metatron and Archangel Seraphiel! I am a part of every Galactic and Multidimensional entity. I may not want or need a tattoo anymore. I feel like it keeps me here but I should do more research on this. I saw my Golden Diamond Rainbow Aura. I met REMEMBER/Victoria, my GDR crystal skull. She helps me remember literally anything. The GDR Ray is mine to wield and using a wand, directs it more intentionally.

I eye-gazed in the mirror longer than I had before and saw myself as different ET blue beings, then my past/future selves, then as my multidimensional vibrational selves. I am NÜ. I am Star.

11/1/21
The Pygmalion Effect
Our whole entire existence happens on the skin of the Earth. The Pleidians also live in the "Inner-Earth" so communication is possible through shadow projection.

-
Shadow Astral Projection Meditation
Intend to project back through your Shadow-Self and see yourself operating in Astral Shadow form. What do you experience?

11/2/21
Trip Log
I had a few chocolates and found one Blue Cloud. As I was taking a shower, animals started showing themselves to me through the stone marble walls. A dolphin was my favorite energy image. The light turned off and I could see black mist coming off of the wall so I got out of the shower. As I got dressed in my room I could feel the pressure like a heavy pulling on my body, which means Beings-Without-Bodies want to

speak with me. I put on a Sirius Portal Star Lionsgate Meditation and we called in all of the Archangels including Archangel Sandalphon. We made an Angel Chamber and they all put their light into me and upgraded all of my energetic bodies. Then the Golden God Beings worked on my eyes!

I was cleaning an item when I was suddenly drawn to the Egyptian painting in the living room. I walked over and looked into the eyes of ISIS and understood she wanted me to decipher the painting, so I did. The patient was a depiction of my enlightenment. I've been given a Seal of the Gods, containing all knowledge and protection. I've been awakened!

I was visited by the Spirit of all Bees and shown how to create a holographic hive for abundance. I love my life! Thank you Ganesh, Archangels, Guides, RoXa and all of my galactic family. I love you!

11/5/21
Dream World
I can feel a pull on my lower Chakras. It is pulling up something heavy and powerful. My higher Chakras keep the higher frequencies in-tune for me. I was wearing a cloak, discussing things with other cloaked Beings. I awaken seeing solar codes, Metatron's Cube with another cube inside and Beings helping me come back. Beings kept talking to me in my dreams at the City Island.

I was back at my grade school. I fell in love again with a childhood love. It felt so real! I wonder what it meant?

-
Dream world
I use my crystals to surround the trauma in Golden Light. Then I heal it with an infinity symbol.

11/11/21

Dream World

I called on the blue beings and they sent little light, fluffy small towel-shaped blue energy to comfort me. I fill myself with blue and teal. Everyone had an elemental girl with them like me. I then became one with the alien entities and they became me. I can create a being within or outside of me. Others can do the same. What color do you want to be?

If I have an item that belongs to someone, I ask, "Who does this belong to?" Concentrate and receive the answer!

11/12/21

Trip Log

Today I found two Blue Clouds. My intentions are to access the 11/11 portal and call in my protection from the galaxy and beyond and to truly connect with and understand my new crystal friends and to know who they are for. Also to get the knowledge and understanding of how to call in guided protection.

From within:
I project
I protect
From within the inside

-

How to Energetically Protect Yourself

To create an energy aura shield of protection, you access your Solar Plexus, Sacral, Root and Heart Chakras. Combine them together at your center about 1 foot/12 inches in front of your chest. With pointed praying hands, point the energy in all directions, spreading and smoothing the Golden Diamond

Rainbow Ray energy all around you, forming a bubble of light to protect you and all who are within it!

11/15/21

I just moved to the beach...and it's amazing!

11/16/21

Dream World

The Lyrans were speaking to me and channeling through me. They have messages for me to deliver... So many downloads and visions come to me now before I fall asleep and as I am waking. Both eyes closed and open.

11/18/21-11/19/21

Blood Moon Lunar Eclipse Meditation Experience

I remembered to look down and I saw my light. I saw the yin and yang energy within me and they activated. I saw myself. My true lightform-self that others see. It was breathtaking. Then I was brought up to the level of the Giant Beings. I met a multi-dimensional being who needed help and also came through the Eclipse Portal! I wish I could explain our interaction but there are no words. Then the multi-dimensional being started interacting with me and it was amazing being accepted and comprehending what and how they operate and exist multidimensionally. So big!

The beings I met were ancient beings that only exist in multi-dimensions but I saw them coming through the Lunar Eclipse Portal. They downloaded information into me and told me ways of how to manifest and also that I am one of them. These beings I had no idea even existed. Now I know who some of the eyes are that I see when I close my eyes. I love these beings so much and I'm not sure when I'll see them again. But I'm thankful for what happened. Thank you Universe!!! I'm remembering! When I was in the ether space after the eclipse meditation, I saw the multi-dimensional DMT realm where "the multiple heads" are but it was empty and just a space so I held the space literally with my mind and that's when the Giant Beings started looking at me and finally communicating.

She looked at me with such intensity and so many emotions being projected to me with indecision, excitement, as if she had never seen a "Me" before. I will call her "RED" as that is my only way to try and comprehend this ancient galactic multi-dimensional being in full-color before my eyes. Multi-dimensional! Multi-multi-dimensional is now an understanding I have seen, encountered, conversed with and now I will live and teach their lesson...LOVE!

11/29/21

I have come into new knowledge of who I am and who I have been and where I have been. I am first and foremost an Arcturian who has been incarnated as an Andromeda, Sirian, Vegan, Pleiadian; essentially I have lived in this multi-verse as everything including the Draconians. I'm realizing that the time when I met my inner-self, it was my Arcturian lightbody-self and they had brought me aboard their light ship. That's why I could see the earth to my left and I could see the hallway with the portals on both sides. Also of the ethereal deck we were "standing" on. OMG greatness! I think I go there during my dream state when I help heal the other souls with color and vibrational technology!

-
Dream World

Andromeda, Haniel, Metatron. I was fully functional in the dream island city.

12/1/21

My dream situations are getting more vivid and intense. I'm now becoming more aware and able within my dreams. I understand now that my dream states are really me traveling to the present time of my other-dimensional-selves and realities in different dimensions. Andromeda is calling me.

12/6/21

"The final instructions will be given at Mount Shasta. I already have all of the healing tools I need. Once the website is up, people will find me through my daily videos. From that I will find my clientele." The "snake" represents sound waves in alchemy. Andromeda is coming.

Dream World

I drink in the frequency of the crystal and I then harness the new vibration and heal with it.

12/9/21

I'm starting to enjoy my sleep/dream life better than my 3D life here. I have been going to the same places and talking to familiar faces and falling in love and many other adventurous things. I'm trying to get my spark back because I want to go back home. I love Urantia but she is hurting and that is hurting me. As I accept my situation and delve into these different realms to bring back knowledge for all, I find myself excited but also sad for some reason. I am strengthening my mind for what is coming. I can feel my abilities are needed!

12/11/21

Last night before sleep I stated that I wanted to go to the Angelic Realm (6D). Shortly after I saw a female face twice, then a curly blonde-haired Being appeared and started talking to me. It startled me and I know it was one of the Archangels.

I'm guessing Michael. Then I saw a beautiful mountain and tree landscapes. I am going deeper...

-

Trip Log
Blue Cloud Level One at 10:30 AM. Thank you for my life, my abundance, everything!

12/21/21
The Green Ray of Life
I finally unlocked my Green Color Spectrum Ray of Life. As soon as I touched my new Sirian Crystal Skull a Portal was instantly activated in the center of the park where I sat. I was unsure on how to create warmth within my body. I focus on the inside of my body and I imagine plant life, very green, sprouting to life and expand on that imagery. This begins to manifest and it creates an internal Sun that I can then send to any part of my body that is cold. This allows me to naturally warm my core and cold points when outside in the cold.

"The Green Ray of Life Creation" is something to be taught and shared with the world. I also received a crystal bracelet that is a portal to all 12 members of the Galactic Federation. I am excited to discover what it will share with me about my intergalactic heritage. It is time to write "The Book." I am ready! I feel ready and the book calls me. My Archangels are guiding me and my crystals and skulls are enhancing me to my maximum unlimited potential.

Justin "Star" Ingram or "Baba NU" is a Bright Light with an exceptional gift.

He is a Psychic Medium/Reiki healer who has taught himself how to "awaken your psychic abilities".

He was born in Pasadena, CA and has always been a psychic empath and oracle. He is the oldest of 9 children and could always feel the emotions of others before anyone else. Friends call him their personal "spirit doctor". He can hear thoughts and see energy so his family always said he was a little weird but that didn't stop him from following his psychic calling.

With a direct, compassionate and humorous approach, Justin provides a coaching style similar to "chatting with a best friend".

Justin says even Spirit has a sense of humor! Justin provides insight into what is happening now and an action plan on which steps should be taken next. Those who are looking to expand their own spiritual gifts often find themselves working with Justin, as he provides the tips and tools to tap in to their own spirit team. Justin Star Ingram calls a session with him "The Ingram Experience" and provides guidance to the new generation.

Website: www.theingramexperience.com
Email: theingramexperience@gmail.com
TikTok: @theingramexperience

www.ingramcontent.com/pod-product-compliance
Lightning Source LLC
Chambersburg PA
CBHW030526130626
46549CB00007B/3110